Nervous Ned

Written by: Sarah Wysocki
Illustrated by: Galih Winduadi

Once there was a boy named Ned, and he often felt like he had snakes squirming in his belly and a runaway train of thoughts in his head. He did not want to feel this way, but he could not help it.

When he went to the park, he would see kids running wild and free and having fun. He desperately wanted to join them, but something in him held him back. He felt nervous and scared.

At the park, he was flooded with worries. *What if I go on the swings and fall off, and everyone laughs at me?* he thought.

What if I go down the slide and get stuck, and all the kids get mad because I caused a traffic jam?

What if I'm on the monkey bars and a real monkey jumps from the trees and starts attacking me?

Wherever Ned went, his mind was filled with worries. When he walked into school, he was faced with a barrage of things that could go wrong.

What if I forget where my classroom is and walk into the wrong room? Just thinking of the possibility made him cringe with embarrassment.

What if I get a drink at the water fountain and it starts spraying like crazy and soaks me? Everyone would make fun of me!

What if I sit at my desk and my bottom gets stuck because someone put glue on my seat? As you can see, worry and embarrassment awaited Ned everywhere he turned.

Ned's parents tried to reassure him that he was safe and what he worried about would never happen. Even though he trusted them, he still could not make his mind stop worrying.

When it was time to go to bed, Ned would feel a familiar panic creep in. His mind raced with all the possible things that could go wrong.

What if Mom was picked up by an alien spaceship in the middle of the night and the aliens forget to return her?

What if my brother stayed in the bathtub too long and turned into a duck?

*What if my dog **wasn't** really a dog but an evil monster that was just waiting to eat me?*

Ned's parents once again reassured him that none of these things would happen, and after what seemed like an eternity of tossing and turning and worrying, he would finally fall asleep.

Ned didn't like that his mind always thought of all the bad things that could happen. Ned wanted to be carefree like the other kids, but his racing mind made it feel like it would never happen.

One day, Ned was in his yard thinking all the things that could go wrong, the big oak tree in front of him could fall on his head or the bird that might swoop down and pluck out his eyes, the invisible killer bugs that he wouldn't even see as they get ready to attack.

Ned had just gone inside when a girl named Lily stopped by. Lily asked Ned if he wanted to play. Lily looked so friendly and seemed so excited that Ned agreed to go back outside.

Lily asked Ned to play hopscotch and took him by the hand. Even though Ned was afraid he would fall down and Lily would laugh, he tried.

Guess what? He didn't fall, and he had fun.

Ned thought about his fun afternoon playing with Lily and how he was worried something bad would happen or she would laugh at him but that didn't happen. He began to think that maybe other things he worried about were not so worrisome after all.

The next day, when he saw kids playing at the park, his same worrisome thoughts came creeping back in. He was afraid something bad was going to happen to him or he would do something embarrassing.

Luckily, Lily was there and took his hand and asked him to swing. He remembered how much fun they had last time they played, so he followed along. In no time, Lily and Ned were swinging high in the sky, laughing the whole way!

It took some time, but slowly, Ned began to realize the things he worried about were pretty silly, and most of them would never happen. Ned started to try to do things that scared him more and more, and each time he tried something scary, he felt a little stronger and braver.

Ned soon began to focus more on the things he wanted and less on things he was afraid of. It took time and practice, but he was determined to try scary things like playing at the park or entering a room full of unfamiliar faces. Sometimes his nervous thoughts still took over, but he always knew he could try again tomorrow.

Author
BIO

As a long-time educator, Sarah Wysocki has seen time and time again the power of a good story. As a child, Sarah loved to get lost in the adventures of her most beloved characters. Her favorite stories were always ones with characters she could relate to particularly little girls who found trouble no matter where they went or how hard they tried to avoid it. As a child, Sarah found trouble easily and often both at home and at school.

The inspiration behind Sarah's writing is to provide entertaining stories where children from all walks of life can see bits of themselves. Sarah knows how powerful stories can be to open the door to important and sometimes tough conversations. That's why she writes about topics that are relevant to kids and important for educators and parents to acknowledge and discuss. Sarah is a parent to two children, an adventurous and brave little girl, and a rough and tumble and sweet little boy. To learn more about Sarah and to see what stories she's cooking up next visit https://sarahwysocki.online

Illustrator
BIO

Galih Winduadi is a professional digital visual artist with experience in illustration, character design, and other digital art productions. He creates fun and colorful images for people all around the world.

Made in the USA
Middletown, DE
15 March 2021